Spot the Differences

Cheetah or Leopard?

by Jamie Rice

Bullfrog Books

Ideas for Parents and Teachers

Bullfrog Books let children practice reading informational text at the earliest reading levels. Repetition, familiar words, and photo labels support early readers.

Before Reading

- Discuss the cover photo. What does it tell them?

- Look at the picture glossary together. Read and discuss the words.

Read the Book

- "Walk" through the book and look at the photos. Let the child ask questions. Point out the photo labels.

- Read the book to the child, or have him or her read independently.

After Reading

- Prompt the child to think more. Ask: What did you know about cheetahs and leopards before reading this book? What more would you like to learn?

Bullfrog Books are published by Jump!
5357 Penn Avenue South
Minneapolis, MN 55419
www.jumplibrary.com

Library of Congress Cataloging-in-Publication Data

Names: Rice, Jamie, author.
Title: Cheetah or leopard? / by Jamie Rice.
Description: Bullfrog books.
Minneapolis, MN: Jump!, Inc., [2022]
Series: Spot the differences
Includes index. | Audience: Ages 5–8
Identifiers: LCCN 2021028656 (print)
LCCN 2021028657 (ebook)
ISBN 9781636903439 (hardcover)
ISBN 9781636903446 (paperback)
ISBN 9781636903453 (ebook)
Subjects: LCSH: Cheetah—Juvenile literature.
Leopard—Juvenile literature.
Classification: LCC QL737.C23 R535 2022 (print)
LCC QL737.C23 (ebook)
DDC 599.75/9—dc23
LC record available at https://lccn.loc.gov/2021028656
LC ebook record available at https://lccn.loc.gov/2021028657

Editor: Jenna Gleisner
Designer: Michelle Sonnek

Photo Credits: Eric Isselee/Shutterstock, cover, 1, 20, 21, 24; Laura Romin & Larry Dalton/Alamy, 3, 8–9; Stu Porter/Shutterstock, 4, 6–7 (bottom); 12–13, 16–17, 23tm, 23bl; RealityImages/Shutterstock, 5; mariusz_prusaczyk/iStock, 6–7 (top); Breaking The Walls/Shutterstock, 10–11; Dr Ajay Kumar Singh/Shutterstock, 14–15, 23tl, 23tr; 1001slide/iStock, 18–19; MOIZ HUSEIN STORYTELLER/Shutterstock, 22 (left); Philippe Clement/Shutterstock, 22 (right); Volodymyr Burdiak/Shutterstock, 23bm; GP232/iStock, 23br.

Printed in the United States of America at Corporate Graphics in North Mankato, Minnesota.

Table of Contents

A cheetah has round spots.
A leopard has rosettes.
Which is this?

How to Use This Book

In this book, you will see pictures of both cheetahs and leopards. Can you tell which one is in each picture?

Hint: You can find the answers if you flip the book upside down!

Big Cats

This is a cheetah.

This is a leopard.

Both are big cats.

They look alike.

But they are
not the same.

Can you spot
the differences?

A cheetah has round spots.

A leopard has rosettes.

Which is this?

A cheetah's face has black lines.

A leopard's face does not.

Which is this?

Answer: cheetah

A cheetah can't roar.

A leopard can.

Which is this?

A cheetah has thin legs.

It chases prey.

A leopard has thick legs.

It stalks prey.

Which is this?

Answer: cheetah

prey

cub

A leopard mom has
two or three cubs.

A cheetah mom
can have up to six.

Which is this?

Nap time!

A cheetah sleeps under a tree.

A leopard sleeps in a tree.

Which is this?

See and Compare

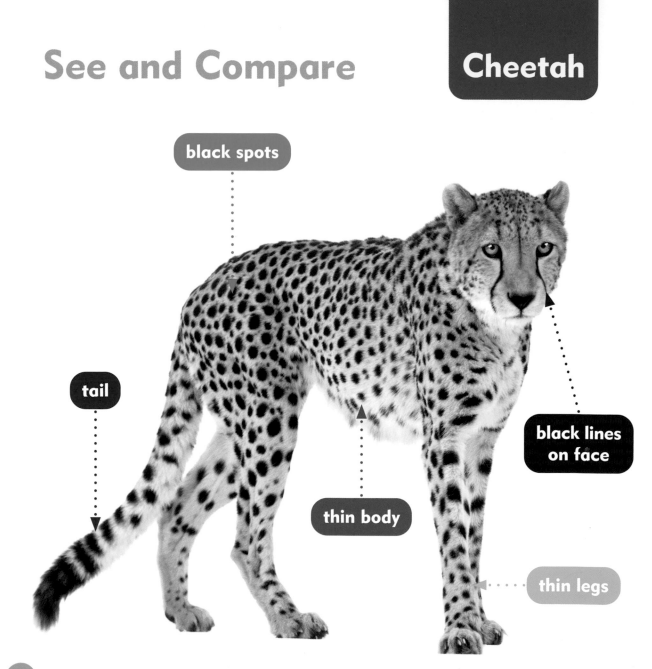

black spots

tail

black lines on face

thin body

thin legs

20

Leopard

black rosettes

tail

thick body

thick legs

Quick Facts

Cheetahs and leopards are both wild cats. They are both mammals. This means they give birth to live young. They are similar, but they have differences. Take a look!

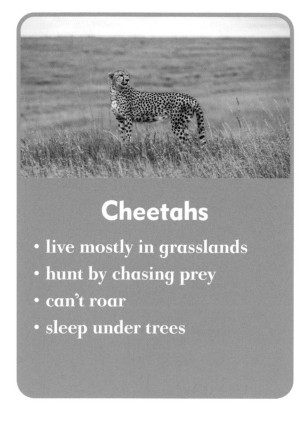

Cheetahs

- live mostly in grasslands
- hunt by chasing prey
- can't roar
- sleep under trees

Leopards

- live in grasslands, rain forests, mountains, and deserts
- hunt by quietly stalking prey
- can roar
- often sleep in trees

Picture Glossary

chases
Runs after something in order to catch it or scare it away.

cubs
Young cheetahs or leopards.

prey
Animals that are hunted by other animals for food.

roar
To make a deep, loud sound.

rosettes
Rose-shaped markings on the fur or skin of some animals.

stalks
Tracks or hunts in a quiet, secret way.

Index

To Learn More

Finding more information is as easy as 1, 2, 3.

❶ Go to www.factsurfer.com

❷ Enter "cheetahorleopard?" into the search box.

❸ Choose your book to see a list of websites.

FACT SURFER